THE
ROMANTIC
LOVER

the
joy of sex

THE
ROMANTIC
LOVER

the
joy*of*sex

The Joy of Sex: The Romantic Lover
by Susan Quilliam

First published in Great Britain in 2009 by Mitchell Beazley,
an imprint of Octopus Publishing Group Limited,
2–4 Heron Quays, London E14 4JP.
An Hachette Livre UK Company
www.hachettelivre.co.uk
www.octopusbooks.co.uk

Distributed in the U.S. and Canada by Octopus Books USA:
c/o Hachette Book Group USA, 237 Park Avenue, New York NY 10017
www.octopusbooksusa.com

ISBN: 978-1-84533-472-7

A CIP record for this book is available from the British Library

Set in Spectrum MT

Colour reproduction in Hong Kong by Fine Arts
Printed and bound in China by Toppan Printing Company, Limited

Commissioning Editor Tracey Smith
Senior Editor Leanne Bryan
Copy-editor Suzanne Arnold
Art Director Tim Foster
Senior Art Editor Juliette Norsworthy
Designer Colin Goody
Jacket Designer Pene Parker
Production Controller Susan Fox

CONTENTS

YOUR ROMANTIC RELATIONSHIP

Falling in love may seem like a dream, but dreams can become reality. And reality can last a lifetime.

Lifetime desire

Passion may provide the initial impulse for sex, but it's romance that keeps passion alive. If you stay tender and affectionate to each other, you will always be eager to make love.

Because romance isn't just hearts and flowers or something the media dreamed up. Research tells us it's a universal — and essential — human emotion, wired into our physiology and designed to keep us and the one we love closely bonded to each other.

So let romance reinforce everything you do. A wake-up hug, loving lunch-hour emails, an evening walk, then supper curled up on the sofa together: these are what lead inevitably into wonderful sex before you fall asleep in each other's arms.

Sex then deepens the bond. Gazing into each other's eyes. Endless kisses and tongue play. A loving massage that ends at the genitals. Gentle lovemaking, on and on, with long pauses where you hear each other's hearts beat.

Not that romantic sex always needs to be gentle — some of the most romantic things can be startling, exciting, and unexpected. A pillow fight leading to noisy, climactic intercourse. Being woken by delicious oral pleasure at 2am, barely remembered in the morning. Holding each other back and back until you finally tumble into orgasm together. Given all these, your connection will stay strong.

To keep the romance alive in your sex life — and the passion alive in your love life — read on. For ideas, instructions, inspiration. For how to seduce each other daily, how to pleasure each other in bed and out of bed, how to always remember how deep your desire is for each other.

As erotic novelist Elinor Glyn once said, "Romance is what turns the dust of everyday life into a golden haze". We all deserve to live so richly.

Laying the foundations

Let's start, then, with the absolute basics: seven romantic building blocks — based on research by anthropologist Gary Chapman — used by loving and intimate couples.

Partners who make their relationships work — in bed and out of it — use these building blocks regularly and happily. It works in reverse. Do these things regularly and happily and you'll lay the foundations both for romance and for desire.

1. **Give attention:** quite simply, your partner needs to be the centre of your world. So do things together. Share projects. Set aside time daily to talk and listen about what you've each experienced — and when apart keep a connection by placing a call or sending a message. In particular, give each other sexual attention. Look, listen, smell, taste, touch. Be constantly fascinated. Make your beloved the erotic focus of your life.

2. **Offer gifts:** give whatever shows you care. No, don't break the bank — surveys prove thought counts more than hard cash — but do find out what treasures and treats your lover likes and then deliver. Plus, gifts matter in bed as well as out of it: flowers to mark the first time you made love, massage oil, an erotic bedside book, a special pleasure toy.

3. **Show pride:** make it very clear that you love what your partner does. Not only through compliments, but by registering their victories — when they've overcome a problem, made a hard decision, stood up for themselves. Especially, show sexual pride — in how good they look, how responsive they are, how they arouse you, every single time. It's arguably as important to say you're proud of your partner as to say you love them.

4. **Take action:** one of the most convincing proofs of love is that you're willing to go the extra mile. So cook that meal. Stay up for the night feed. Take the cat to the vet. In sex, be prepared sometimes to give more

than you get — a full-body massage, long oral pleasuring that leaves the other spent, lovemaking the way your partner likes it even if it's not your own favourite style.

5. **Make contact:** touch — always and everywhere. This doesn't just mean foreplay — it's the skin-on-skin contact as well as the arousal that keeps you close. (When 200 women were asked to choose hypothetically between having orgasms and cuddles in their lives, they chose the cuddles.) So take your partner's hand, sit next to them rather than across, kiss hello and goodbye. Don't hold back from being sensual even when there's no chance to follow through; when there is a chance, be as sexual as you can as often as you can.

6. **Build memories:** of course you'll share romantic reminiscences — how you met, when you realized you were in love, your first Christmas, your last holiday. But make memories too of your passionate times. Take photos. Keep souvenirs. Write a daily sex journal — just

two sentences will do, preferably one written by each of you. Be Leonardo di Caprio in *Titanic* and draw your beloved. (It really doesn't matter if you can't draw.)

7. **Create dreams:** plan, and regularly review, your future together — what you'll be doing, where you'll be living, how you'll be together in the years to come. Sexually, too, make plans — for new locations, new positions, new experiences. Never ever settle for "routine"; never ever settle for "enough". In love as well as in life, there is always more to aim for.

A reminder

Of course you remembered, but here's a prompt. Until you've both been tested for infections, you should protect yourselves with condoms for intercourse, oral sex, anal sex, and sex toys.

And unless you're ready to bring up a child you should also use reliable contraception.

SETTING
THE SCENE

Being romantic is about
being private. Withdraw to your
own space — no distractions,
no intrusions. Focussing on
romance means focussing
on each other completely.

The time

The right moment for romantic sex is often now. Over breakfast, walking in the park, dining at your favourite restaurant, or watching a funny film in your own living room, you look across at each other and know you have to make love, no hesitation.

That said, there are best times. Best for him is in the morning, when energy and hormones peak; for her, late evening, when her skin is most sensitive and she's undistracted. (She may also have a best time of the month, two weeks after her period, when the selfish gene is urging her on.) Work with these times; note them, mark them. Above all, take advantage of them.

If, in the daily rush, you don't find any time for sex, stop and wonder why. If there seems no problem that needs a solution, then carve out time regardless; diarize if you have to, even if only for cuddling and conversation. You never know — it may go further.

If life still seems determined to block you, stop again and think. Making love is not just an indulgence, it's a necessity — for health, happiness, and sanity. However important your career, however precious your family, they'll benefit from your having a rich sexual life.

The place

Most romantic sex happens in the privacy of your own home. Because romantic — as opposed to raunchy — is about seclusion; you instinctively withdraw to your own bedroom, or at the least your own hotel room.

So make your setting secluded. Create cocooning through lighting with a log fire or lamps on a dimmer. Candles, though clichéd, will have the same effect and you can also get scented ones. (Remember to place them in bowls of water so they'll extinguish themselves if you're otherwise engaged and too distracted to keep an eye on them.)

No separations: the sofa should be easily long and wide enough to take the two of you full-length. Add a mirror so that wherever you look you bring yourselves back into the here and now; stand in front of it, full on, together and look at yourselves as a couple. (Later, leave the mirror in place and watch yourselves coupling.)

In the bedroom, particularly, ban the workstation and the television – unless it's used to play romantic DVDs. The bed, it goes without saying, should be double not twin; you need to be able to connect at any time during the night.

Cocoon further with bed drapes. Historically this was one of the points of the four-poster bed with curtains, though you can get almost the same effect with hangings of the thin, mosquito-net variety.

For texture, add sheets of silk or cotton on the bed, a velvet drape on the sofa, a rug on the floor. Plus a good set of pillows for sleeping well (make sure one of these is hard enough to slide under her buttocks when needed).

Wherever you play, the temperature level – of course – should be high enough for you to be comfortably naked and fall asleep that way. For an extended session, it's a nice touch to programme the heating so that if you wake in the night you can take another bout on top of the covers rather than huddled underneath them.

Romance away

Once outside the bedroom and into location shots, you may think romance depends on exoticism; the Eiffel Tower – or, better still, the Taj Mahal – seems romantic whereas one's own sitting room may not be.

There's truth in that. And not just emotionally, either, but also on the level of hormones – studies suggest that novelty kick-starts adrenalin and the resulting excitement translates into arousal. (Hence the effect of those adrenalin-sparking roller-coaster rides or the drive in a fast car that leaves you feeling both weak at the knees and flooded with desire.)

But you don't actually need to travel far or go to a fairground. Try sitting in a candlelit summer garden at midnight and find yourselves kissing. Make snow angels during a winter walk and then roll into each other's arms. Pull over on the road to catch a stunning sunset view and then reach out for each other.

All of these romantic feasts can be enjoyed on your own doorstep; the only secret is to keep constantly spotting the opportunity and taking the time to take advantage of it.

If you go truly al fresco, of course, take a little care —
check local laws, though in general if you can't be
seen, you should probably be arrest-proof. While lust
may thrive on danger, romance doesn't — you need
to be safe enough to genuinely lose awareness of the
external world and lose yourselves in each other.
Avoid, therefore, anything that even hints of unsafe.

Actually, in the end, the major criterion for your
choice of romantic location is simple. When you
open your eyes after orgasm, you should see beauty.

Food and drink

It's no coincidence that eating and sex go together;
the parts of the brain controlling both appetites are
linked, so when one physical response gets stirred,
so does the other.

But also, the connection's bedded into our culture as
part of the romance ritual, a wish to look after each

other, a statement of loving intent. So book that
atmospheric restaurant or stay in and cook together.

Cook what? Foods with luxury associations — the trio
of caviar, champagne, and chocolate — are a good
baseline for a starter relationship. If you have history,
choose foods that hold memories — the first meal
you ever had together, the meal you were eating
when he proposed.

But don't limit the range. Anthropologist Helen
Fisher suggests that gastronomic variety kickstarts
arousal. That's also true culturally; even the humble
potato was regarded as an aphrodisiac when first
introduced as a novelty from America to Europe.

Nowadays, in fact, we know that no food is reliably
aphrodisiac in the amounts you can safely eat it in.
But many foods have sensual links so trigger arousal.
Fresh fish or tomatoes straight off the plant smell
like her juices. Whipped cream recalls his semen.

The process, too, can be arousing. Eat "at" each other, holding eye contact while you devour asparagus dipped in butter or any food that involves licking your fingers. Feed each other – strawberries dipped in chocolate are standard and delicious; ring the changes with grapes dipped in honey or a tub of the best ice cream and no spoon. (But be wary of food in the vagina because it can cause infection or oily foods near condoms because they rot the rubber.)

Pass slices of fruit from one mouth to the other – in the film *Tampopo* they passed a raw egg yolk back and forth until it burst. The only way to eat a mango together is in the bath.

Drinking may also be on the menu – clink glasses to add the missing fifth sense of sound to the four already present in the custom of looking, touching, smelling, and then tasting a glass of wine. Argentines insist on eye contact as they clink – absent that, they say, you are condemned to seven years of bad sex.

Alcohol itself will kickstart Nature's aphrodisiac testosterone in both of you – the peak point is apparently two hours after the first glass, which is handily about the length of time it takes to get through the meal and into the bedroom.

Without wanting to be a spoilsport, however, a reminder: romance diminishes in direct proportion to the number of glasses consumed. As the porter in *Macbeth* famously says: "Drink provokes the desire but takes away the performance".

Getting dressed

For her, in particular, clothes are central to the scene-setting. Romantic wrapping makes her erotically conscious of her body: the classic corset pulls her in and holds her as though in an embrace, the shape of suspenders under her skirt keeps her attention where it needs to be.

Her choices, however — male lingerie buyers note —
are typically more romantic than raunchy; if in
doubt, buy pink and cream for her rather than
red and black .

He, meanwhile, is genetically programmed to be
turned on visually. He'll respond most to her shape,
so define it: key items of romantic clothing such as
high-heeled shoes, figure-hugging dresses and waist
chains work because they emphasize what makes
her look most like a woman. Choose for emphasis
on curves and it will play well all around.

Choose too for discreetly obvious access. A top
with lacing begging to be undone, panties with side-
ribbons — these hit the mark not only because of
their practicality but also because they focus your
minds from the start on the logical next step. Poet
Philip Larkin was right when he said that the most
erotic word in the English language is "unbutton".

Sound and music

Whereas vision is his arousal sense, hearing is hers —
it was author Isabelle Allende who commented that
a woman's G-spot is in her ears. But for both of you,
a lover's voice will catch attention more than any
sound other than a baby's cry; if that voice says your
name, the reaction will be even more compelling.

So talk and listen as central to the lead-in. Phone
each other during the day. Talk love-talk when you
meet. Browse the bookshelves (or the web) and get
erotica to read aloud during the lead-in to love —
choose together to be sure you both like it.

Choose together, too, the music you have as
background. Not too lyrical — words distract from the
business at hand in a way that wordless tunes don't.
Not too loud — you want to be able to hear your own
voices even when you're only murmuring. Not too
fast — music played at fewer than 60 beats a minute

relaxingly slows your heart rate, breathing, and blood pressure and so prepares you for lovemaking.

Research suggests the best backdrop to sexual romance is light jazz, new age, Mozart, and Chopin. But you'll have your own favourites that will trump any guidelines. "Our song" is always the best song.

The sexual summons

Truly romantic sex is seldom ordered up instantly. Even when it feels spontaneous, we've usually been sending out intimacy invitations hours – often days – before the event.

Whether you are new partners or a long-established couple, when you want sexual connection, you use body language to say, "I want you… do you want me?" Neglect that dialogue and passion simply never happens. Pursue the conversation and you'll hear a "yes".

Begin, then, with eye contact; turn your regulation-courteous two-second gaze into a longing half-minute to immediately create rapport. (Arthur Aron of the University of New York got students staring into each other's eyes for four minutes. All the subjects reported feeling close. Two of them ended up married.)

Smile genuinely and you add motivation to arousal. If you smile, you show approval; if the other person feels approved of, they feel safe; once they feel safe, they want to get closer; reciprocally, you'll then want to get closer to them.

Once closer, within the intimate zone of six inches, the probability of sensual contact soars. At that point, reach out. Studies show that before sexual contact, couples typically touch a few times much more neutrally: so let your bodies brush as you step past, let your hands graze briefly when you hand a glass from one to the other.

Dancing for love

Don't panic. Whether or not you're a good dancer is absolutely not the point here — although if you're doing public performance dancing for a special occasion, such as the traditional first-on-the-floor at your own wedding, it's wise to practise first or even take a lesson.

Dancing for one another, though, isn't about performance but relationship — not about who is looking at you but how you are looking at each other. Dancing displays each of you for the other, shows what you're "offering", shows you what you are being "offered". (So, quite simply, move your body and be confident.)

Dancing puts you in touch with your desires and gets you anticipating what is to come. There are few things more arousing than a lover walking around the table to take your hand, bring you to your feet, and lead you into the dance.

And then, something even more magical happens. As you move closer and touch, your physiology falls into synchrony not only because you're following a single beat but also because you're following each other.

The "mirroring" that's a sign of deepest rapport happens naturally when you dance with a lover. All you need do is follow their movements on the conscious level and in the end you'll unconsciously fall into step with them, but also with their breathing, heartbeat, blood pressure.

Such connection isn't just arousing foreplay. It's also the perfect preparation for sex; the physiological conversation gives you an unspoken connection that carries over wordlessly into the bedroom.

To which aim, at least when in private, dance as unclothed as you can. Skin on skin, the stimulation as you move enhances the awareness of each sensation; the coming together and moving apart in time to the music sets up a rhythm for lovemaking.

GETTING CLOSER

You walk toward the edge
of intimacy together. So how
best to reach out and connect,
how best to cross the bridge
and find each other?

The compelling scent

As we finally draw closer, it's our natural perfume that most instinctively draws us toward intimacy. Pheromones are nature's way of checking out compatibility; once that's established, they're then nature's way of reminding us of the bond.

So, barring illness, a beloved partner's smell will not only relax you, but will trigger romantic memories; no surprise then that getting close enough to actually smell each other is so often a prelude to sex. So try to offer your own signature scent as you come into each other's arms.

Yes, wash away the gathered daily smells of work and general life. But don't add too many cosmetic smells as a replacement for everyday grime – perfume layered on body lotion layered on deodorant will at best distract from and at worst completely neutralize your individual attractants.

If you do follow Coco Chanel's advice that one should use perfume wherever one wants to be kissed, she in particular could usefully add in a dab of her own genital scent on top of the commercial one for extra effect. (Yes, it may go against all the current deodorized norms, but research suggests it really does work. Try it, at least.)

The scent connection made, the unconscious decision can be taken: proceed or not proceed. At this point new lovers decide whether to make their romantic move; established lovers decide whether to make the time, space, and energy for love.

Five kisses

It was actress Ingrid Bergman who said, "A kiss is a lovely trick designed by nature to stop speech where words become superfluous".

She was only part-right; Polynesians rub noses because they think kissing is weird. But for most of us this particular trick is the first step in seriously declaring our intentions. Here are five ways it can be played out.

1. **The hand kiss**: used – usually by him – to test willingness. The historical custom may have seemed polite formality but was actually a seduction check. If he kisses the palm and adds a hint of tongue to remind her of what a similar organ can do, it can bring even an experienced woman to orgasm.

2. **The cheek kiss**: not the "hello-goodbye" type – which can be shared with anyone – but the one used by her early on in the process to encourage his continuing seduction. Classically she raises her hand to his cheek, then follows with her partly closed mouth, slowly, gently, affectionately. "I'm interested", is her message to him, "so keep trying".

3. **The open-mouth kiss:** checking out whether a prospective partner "tastes right". Get through this test and the selfish gene first primes him with testosterone, then urges him to pass it on in handy, saliva-packaged doses. Kissing, quite simply, is nature's way of dosing both of you up with her own "little blue pill".

4. **The tongue kiss:** entwining , exploring, arousing; introduce just one finger into your mouth as you kiss to add interest to the game. English-speaking lovers call this a "French kiss"; modern Gauls call it "soul kissing". The latter version is nicer.

5. **The penetrating kiss:** where both tongues reflect what will happen later. Note to eager males: don't go too hard; only one in 10 women likes urgent and thrusting, though she's likely to be more willing the more aroused she is. When "later" happens, and he's inside, she can call the pace with her tongue in his mouth.

How to touch

Interesting thought: the natural itinerary of seduction – from outside in, from extremities to centre line – is also, uncoincidentally, the natural order of romantic sex. Moving from hands to face to shoulders to arms and then working your way down; never so swiftly it's threatening, never so slowly it loses momentum.

Breasts provide a natural halfway stop; genitals are the final destination. But never go straight there; as in the rest of life, it's the detours that create the best journeys.

Fingers and lips are the basic tools of your trade, but explore any combination possible. Arms encircling to place hands on nipples as you pass, a foot stretched across to rest on genitals as you sit and talk. Surely deep intimacy means every body part is available to every other.

And surely no kind of touch should ever be out of bounds. Stroke, rub, scratch, graze, tap, pat. Yes, in general she'll like it more delicate and uncertain while he'll prefer more firm and sure — but that can change in the heat of the moment. Given that your hands can do it and your partner is willing, everything is worth trying at least once.

Love wrestling

If you're not in the mood for gentle, here's an alternative: forceful.

This doesn't mean aggressive. It may start with light teasing, a joking insult, or affectionate sarcasm. From there it's a short step to puppy playfulness — one of you throws something soft and a few minutes later, hormones pumping, and halfway between laughter and passion, you find you're both somehow on the floor.

Don't hold back — actively cultivate this. It's a different sort of foreplay but — particularly if you need a release of tension — sometimes even more effective than the seductive kind. Moreover, if you're in a sexual rut or find it difficult to initiate desire, this energy-raising approach can often be the best way in.

Only two guidelines: first, neither of you should immediately overpower the other completely or the fun's half gone. Second, no viciousness, or the fun will disappear completely.

Instead, aim always for connection. Try locking hands and simply pushing against each other. Try intertwining your legs and then resisting. Even tickling can arouse you if it connects you — there are, apparently, 70,000 members of the web-based Tickling Forum and their site suggests numerous ways this particular game can be highly erotic.

At the end, take it into the bedroom. Whoever wins the pillow fight gets a massage. Whoever loses gives the other oral pleasure. Don't think romance is always about affection and tenderness. It is a lot of the time. But it can also be about energy and strength.

Getting naked

Yes, of course you can have sex without taking your clothes off. (It's what lovers in almost every culture do if they aren't ready – or allowed – to go further. If you can't undress fully, it's exciting to just fondle and thrust fully clothed.)

But most of us make love undressed and that's exactly how it should be. Getting naked not only makes you feel freer and more intimate. It also, in a culture that thinks everyone else looks picture-perfect and we don't, shows trust. Undressing for a lover is an act of faith as well as an act of arousal.

It's worth remembering, as you undress, that the original striptease artist was a goddess — Inann, who at each of the seven gates to the underworld removed one veil. That feeling of reverence should hold true even when — perhaps especially when — you're an established couple who've seen it all so many times before.

So go slowly, keeping eye contact, making your audience wait, showing some attitude.

She starts from the top and works down — turning sideways to show off her curves. When it comes to her bra, she lowers the straps, then holds the cups across her breasts for a moment to build suspense before removing it.

Stockings can be tricky if she's not used to them — she rolls them off with both hands, slips them off her heels, then holds them in finger and thumb before setting them down. The suspenders follow, then the knickers, with two hands sliding them over her hips — she lets them fall to the floor then steps out.

Of course, she should follow the example of *Kama Sutra* women by keeping all her jewellery on even when all her clothes are off.

He, meanwhile, starts from the feet and works up — socks first, please, or risk looking silly. He can "present", too, if he likes, standing full on to look solid and strong and saving his shirt till last so that the final removal reveals his whole torso in all its glory.

Of course if, rather than undressing for each other, you are undressing each other, that's very different. Yes, follow the pattern of top down for her and bottom up for him. But make it gentle, nurturing, with affection rather than with attitude. Stand back and look admiringly. Offer compliments. Kiss. Caress. Make it very, very safe.

Mapping pleasure

Taking an inventory of each other's most sensitive areas: a good starting point for all new lovers and a good revision exercise for established ones.

Is it vital? After all, every sex manual lists out the regulation erogenous zones and surely it's just a question of working your way down the list?

The problem is, such catalogues seriously miss the point. Everyone has their own infinitely personalized sensitivities and any partner who isn't just painting-by-numbers needs to find out what plays best.

Yes, do it informally, as you go. But, equally, it's nice sometimes to be formal, to tell your beloved to lie still for a while then, as the eighteenth-century diarist Ananda Ranga suggests, to touch them absolutely everywhere.

And not only those places rich in nerve endings, such as lips, earlobes, feet, buttocks, breasts, and genitals. Also explore the least used and so most sensitive zones: the eyelids, inner elbows, behind the knee, the nape of the neck, the crease under her breasts, or the tender spot just under his testicles.

After which, also check places you absolutely can't imagine being sensitive and prepare to be surprised. Some women can orgasm through firm touch on the big toe alone and Tantric masters say that stimulating the upper lip boosts sensitivity everywhere else. Don't take any of this on trust; in this game, the only worthwhile knowledge is self-taught.

Don't, either, regard the knowledge-learning as dusted once done. Erogenous zones change from day to day, month to month (for her), and even from start to end of lovemaking. Keep checking.

Also, keep communicating. Tell your beloved when something holds your attention, so that they can do it more. This will bring out the best in your lover.

ROMANTIC MASSAGE

Relaxing, winding down, stroking, soothing; this is the perfect preparation for love.

Bathing together

Every sex guide recommends it to the point of cliché: the sensual bath complete with aromatherapy oils and tea candles. But there's a truth lurking here. Bathing with someone you love, skin-on-skin and surrounded by warm water, is a fundamental trigger. You feel secure, "back in the womb".

It's both nurturing and arousing — a natural transition from daily life into erotic pleasure. (If you want to know how erotic, remember that early Christians denounced the perfumed bath as a sin.)

You could follow the Japanese custom. Use the shower to wash — including each other's hair — then snuggle together in warm towels while the tub fills with water as hot as you can stand it. Then use the bath not to clean but to soak luxuriously, emerging stress-free to shift seamlessly into lovemaking.

(Given a high enough bank balance, you could also
do what celebrities Johnny Depp and Kate Moss
allegedly did and fill the tub with champagne; just
be careful your maid doesn't pull the plug, like theirs
did, and lose the lot.)

Shower heads can be used all over but particularly
on nipples and genitals; if she can't normally take
too much clitoral stimulation this will play well –
to soften it even further, use the shower head
underwater in the bath. (Steer clear of her vagina,
however – fluid under pressure can damage.)

Lovemaking in the bath itself only really works if
you have a huge tub – the best position is her-on-
top; otherwise settle for one of you staying outside
the bath and paying attention to the one sitting in it.

As for the previously mentioned aromatherapy
oils and candles, they actually do perform; aromas
and low light relax, sensitize, and prepare you for

arousal. But use the oils with care: her vagina or his glans may be delicate and nothing is less erotic than itching or scratching.

As to candles, you could do well to emulate the man who showed his lover into a bathroom filled with hundreds of lighted candles, a tub full of bubbles, and a pair of beautiful earrings strung from a length of ribbon and dangling over the bath.

If this scenario is a gift from her to him, you could replace the gift of earrings dangling over the bath with her already lying in it and willing to oblige.

Body paint

Traditionally a sexual decoration – genital tattooing for a Fijian pubescent girl, henna mehndi hand-dyeing for an Indian bride. The West threw a disapproving tantrum about two thousand years ago, until — perhaps with the arrival of reliable in-house heating — we remembered what fun it is to decorate our own skin. Since cosmetics artist Max Factor bodypainted a model at the 1933 World Fair, we've not looked back.

What you use depends on your motive. For sheer decoration — followed by lots of admiring in the mirror — body paint offers more colours; they now even do them glittery and glow-in-the-dark. For sheer eroticism and a quick road into mouthwork, however, flavoured edible paints would be your medium of choice. Art shops or online stores will supply the former; the latter were originally sex-store specials but at holiday time now feature heavily as couple presents.

Set up in a bathroom, shower room, or private garden; otherwise, put down plastic sheeting and replaceable towels. Use a small brush or sponge for detail and bigger brushes or your fingers, palms, feet, buttocks, or breasts for daubing. Genitals can daub, too — try his penis in her hand — but do a patch test first and avoid putting paint into body orifices.

Don't worry about getting arty — you're not painting the *Mona Lisa* here. Simply beautify your beloved and yourself and get to play some nice skin games at the same time.

Draw patterns, shapes, names, flowers. Enjoy touching and being touched. Then enjoy washing or licking it all off again.

Making preparations

Massage is a great new-lover seduction technique; if you both end up naked and oiled the next step is practically inevitable. It's also an unparalleled lead-in for established partners: nurturing, relaxing, stress-reducing. All serious lovers should exchange a romantic massage at least monthly.

So how to prepare? The most fundamental detail is a firm underpinning — the floor or bed rather than the sofa — plus a softer layer on top: a quilt, sheet, or bath towel. Again, choose nothing you'd miss if it got ruined: oil is often uncontrollable even if all you do is massage.

For the main task, your own hands — newly washed and with the fingernails well clipped — are the essential tools.

Massage oil has moved from being exotic to being sold everywhere: pharmacies, health food shops — even your local petrol station probably has a full range. Avoid over-scented oils unless you're sure neither of you is allergic to them.

If the oil isn't in an easy-pour bottle, transfer it to something more convenient — being able to replenish the oil in your hand during massage without breaking stride is the mark of a true expert.

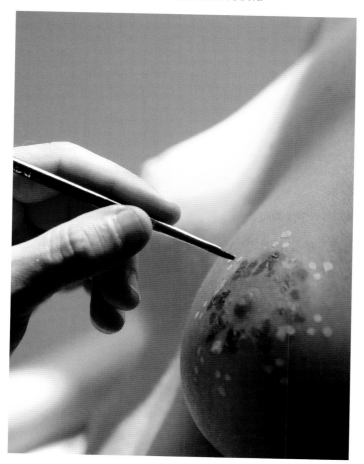

Massage variations

The above preparations are the basics for simple hand-on-skin massage, the main course of any such banquet. But of course you can vary the menu.

Other textures, in particular, can add both interest and effectiveness. It's probably best not to introduce them with a new partner or one who hasn't already been forewarned. But if you are an established couple, both at ease with each other, you may want to experiment.

First option: a massage glove. I've seen them in fur, satin, velvet — they're good for initial soothing and smoothing, to prepare the skin for more in-depth pressure. If you are caught unprepared, wind a silk scarf several times around the fingers of one hand; long hair used similarly is a nice alternative.

Gloves also come in knobbly rubber and leather with prickly studs; you need to take care with the latter to avoid over-exfoliating the skin and some people simply find them uncomfortable or distracting.

You can now also buy a whole collection of massage implements: wheels, brushes, balls. Some of these can be warmed, for deeper muscle relaxation. Use very lightly for all-over body sensations, or more directly wherever you would use your thumbs, knuckles or elbows.

Plus, there are so-called massage vibrators – which, of course, despite innocent advertising, are really intended for more advanced games, though they're also surprisingly good for actual massage.

A nice alternative for light touching is to use feathers – use soft ones such as peacock for all-body brushing and stiff wiry ones for more arousing touching on the soles of the feet or nipples. Gentle trailing with a feather boa, a silk stocking, or even a flower can be a lovely way to start a session.

Massage strokes

Of course it's passion, not skill, that makes a lover's touch welcome. For massage, however, things go better if the one doing the work also has expertise. So here's a list of basic movements and then a step-by-step guide.

If you are both novices, it'll also help to be massaged by someone who already knows what they're doing; then you can try the moves on each other at home to see what you prefer. If you get really keen, you can also take courses.

The usual way to work is with the palms of your hands, fingertips, and — gently — thumbs. But you can also use the side of the hand; some masseurs use knuckles, elbows, or the flat of the forearm for attacking deep, strong muscles.

Here's the safety code. Don't: grab, slap, or massage on bone or over organs near the surface. Avoid: scars, varicose veins, cuts, bruises, injuries, damaged blood vessels, or the abdomen if she's pregnant. Check with a health professional if the massagee has any chronic or acute condition or is taking medication, particularly blood thinners.

I've seen entire catalogues of 80 types of massage movements; this shortlist is just a starter menu.

1. Slide palms over skin.

2. Knead muscles with fingers or thumbs.

3. Scratch delicately with fingernails.

4. Tap lightly with fingertips, a move known as "spiders' feet" or *pattes d'araignée*.

5. Use soft chops on the back, thigh, and calf, a move known as "tapotage".

6. Make small, circling movements with knuckles or elbow.

7. Place hands flat and slide them upward, then pull back down in one stroke.

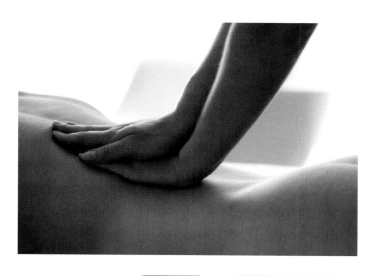

8. Hold both hands parallel, horizontal, and with the fingers pointing in; slide both clockwise in a circular motion, allowing the lower hand to pass under the upper one and then drop back down. (This "circle stroke" is easier to perform than to describe.)

Step by step

A full-body massage takes well over an hour; it can also leave the practitioner exhausted. So you may want to do it piecemeal; you may, too, want to leave time for both of you to take turns. Here are the instructions.

Keep the room warmer than you think you'll need; you're moving but your massagee isn't and so may get cool. If they are unclothed, cover the part you're not massaging with a towel.

Keep your attention constantly on your partner to sense what they are feeling; pace your movements to their rate of breathing and as they unclench and their breathing slows, slow your movements, too.

Always work both sides of the body and, wherever you can, massage up the limbs toward the heart.

Never take both hands away, even when replenishing oil; it may break your partner's mood. Instead, have oil within easy reach and, when it's needed, leave one hand, palm up, resting on your partner's skin and pour the oil into that palm.

Begin with your partner on their front and sit or kneel beside them. Place one hand on their back and breathe with them.

If they are stressed, get them to tense then relax each part of their body in turn, from the feet up to the head and out to the hands (*see* page 90 for more detail).

When massaging, sit beside your partner or straddle with your weight off them. For face or foot massage, sit at right angles to their body, looking along it.

Begin by making several long strokes from the base of the spine to the top of the head. Then include any or all of the following.

Back massage: pinch gently, moving from the shoulders in to neck. Stroke the entire back area with flat palms. Press with your knuckles on the muscles on each side of the spine and the small of the back.

Leg and foot massage: rub the feet briskly with the palms of your hands, then make small circles on the soles with your knuckles – not so soft that it tickles, but not so hard that it hurts. Stroke or knead up the calf and thigh muscles, then knead the buttocks with your knuckles or elbows.

Head massage: if it's acceptable to get oil on your partner's hair, massage their scalp with your fingertips. Stroke along the forehead, down the nose, across the cheeks, and along the jaw line. Rub the ears and earlobes. Steer well clear of eyes.

Chest massage: stroke with flat palms down your partner's chest and out to their breasts. Circle the nipples — no tweaking.

Hand and arm massage: use pressure with your thumb on the palm. Hold each separate finger in a fist and pull it lightly. Stroke or knead arm muscles upward toward the shoulder.

Stomach massage: use the "circle stroke" to make round movements, palm over palm. Always go clockwise and very gently, so as not to disturb your partner's digestion.

End your massage by sitting alongside your partner again and making more long, slow strokes down from their shoulders past their genitals and on down to their feet.

Then leave your hands on your partner for several minutes, breathing with them. Then decide what comes next.

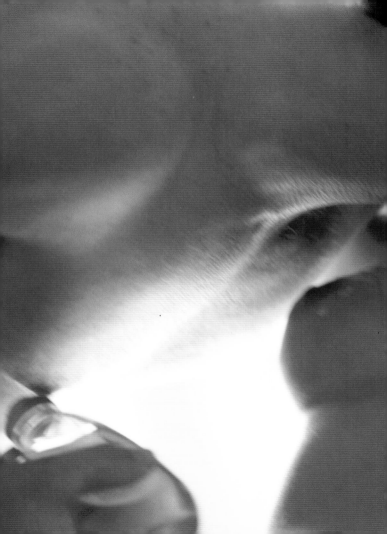

On to passion

The end point of all the above doesn't have to be sexual, but for romantic lovers it often is. It's such an easy transition from using hands for massage to using them to arouse – and an even easier step then to include mouth and tongue work.

Start the slide into erotic with extremities such as earlobes and toes, then gradually work your way inward. Keep it soft and rhythmic until you reach the genitals; then gradually begin to heat things up.

For an unforgettable finale, try this. Oil yourself well. Then, with the massagee on their stomach, lower yourself down along the length of their body, with your weight on your hands; if it's him massaging her, his penis should be on her back rather than distractingly nudging her buttocks. Then, simply slither up and down. (This, allegedly, was Marilyn Monroe's signature move; the friction would bring her to climax – and presumably it didn't leave her partner unaffected, either.)

To continue to intercourse, turn the massagee onto their back and get well-lubricated genitals involved. Gentle penetration, please, or you'll break the receiver out of their massage trance; and go easy on the oil or there won't be sufficient friction to make the moves worthwhile. (Remember, too, that some oils destroy condoms.)

With penetration, you're performing what Tantric sources call internal massage; for best effect, what's suggested is a long, slow, shifting series of thrusts: nine shallow plus one deep, eight shallow plus two deep, and so on until all thrusts are deep.

Bring things to a conclusion with cocooning, both of you wrapped in a soft towel or quilt and cuddled up together. A hot soapy shower to wash off the oil completes the ritual.

EMOTIONAL CONNECTION

Whatever you feel, this is
a safe place to share it. You
will be accepted. Open your
hearts to each other.

First thoughts

When teaching that most romantically sexual of dances, the tango, the best instructors tell students to ignore the complex positions and figures. Only two things are important in the dance, they say: presence and connection.

Presence means being truly there, in the moment, free of physical interruptions and emotional distractions. Connection means being fully engaged with your partner, having absolute attention for them and what they are doing.

Which seems a fair assessment of what's needed for romantic sex. It's not enough only to turn up; you have to check the rest of your life in at the door. It's not enough to lie in the same bed as your partner; you must lie with them in the deepest sense of the words.

What follows in this chapter is a menu of suggestions for doing just that.

Breathing together

If you've survived the day from hell — or even
another standard week — then taking time to
simply breathe together will calm you.

So settle — preferably facing each other and with
your backs straight. Perhaps standing, arms around
each other. Or each one seated at either end of the
couch, feet touching. Best, claim Eastern mystics, is
with him cross-legged, her in his lap with her legs
around his waist, genitals barely touching.

Then, together, three deep, stress-releasing
inhalations. After that, breathe as normal. Don't try
to breathe in unison, just do what feels comfortable.
Yes, if you sense your partner's pattern changing, go
with that if you want — but not if you don't want to.

In the end, quite naturally, no time limit, you'll
fall into sync. Let that happen. Quieten all the way
down. You're here, home, with each other.

Relaxing together

Tense bodies don't make good love. If you need
to seriously unwind before sex, try this.

Lie flat on your backs on the floor or a firm sofa —
next to each other if you like — and take a moment
to settle. Then, in turn, tense and relax every muscle
in your body, one by one.

Hands first, then arms, shoulders, neck, face (open
and close your mouth a few times to release the jaw),
then back muscles, buttocks, stomach, thighs,
calves, feet, toes.

For each, allow five seconds of tension and 10 seconds
of relaxation, then move on to the next body area.
If you can't get a feel for how quickly time passes,
count "one elephant… two elephants" and so on.

When you're done — it may take one of you longer
than it takes the other — lie still for a while and enjoy
the feeling of relaxation.

Calming the mind

Making love with sensitivity means focussing not outward on the everyday world but in on the sexual moment, not thinking about then and there but concentrating absolutely on here and now.

So take a moment to look at your partner — no matter if they're not looking at you. Note their features, every detail, sharp and distinct. Recall, if you want, poet Edwin Muir's moving line, "Yours, my love, is the right human face".

And listen to the sounds around you, from outside the room, from inside the room, from you and your partner breathing.

Then turn your attention to your body and how it feels — warm, cold, heavy, light, balanced, still, shifting. And to your partner's body and exactly where it is — touching yours, pressing on yours, separate from it. Let your mind go quiet. Simply, be.

Those in the know will recognize this exercise as a form of meditation. It's fine if you don't want to think of it that way — though you may want to bear in mind that those who practise meditation often enjoy better, more orgasmic and more long-lasting sex.

Releasing emotions

Sometimes what lovers feel isn't all hearts and flowers, but thorns among the roses. It's still romance.

Because intimacy is about authenticity. If you're going to be real with each other in bed, you have to be real outside the bedroom, authentic when you're sad, anxious, even irritated — about your everyday life and even about each other.

This isn't psychobabble, even if it is psychological. Scientists now tell us that love is a primitive human emotion — on the same level as the central three of

grief, fear, and anger. Refuse to feel those three and
you lose capacity for all four. Sometimes the way to
feel good enough to enjoy sex is by facing the fact
that you feel bad.

Sadness: facing up to sorrow is easier for her than it is for
him; despondency is seen as weakness for most men.
But when there's sadness in our lives, the best solution
for everyone is to express it — because tears contain
a natural painkiller, release stress hormones, and
help us to relax.

Plus, showing sadness attracts support; our partner
comforts us, and that helps us feel better. It also
strengthens the bond; a hug works for the one giving
as well as the one getting.

To follow, sex isn't just comforting but also life-
affirming, the strongest of statements that whatever
loss you've suffered, you survive. Which is why it's not
sick but sensible if you find yourselves responding to

even major life losses by making love. It's perfectly possible – sometimes completely appropriate – to have passionate sex with tears rolling down your face.

Anxiety: worry, too, will be difficult for him to express; men are supposed to cope with life's challenges. But studies show that it helps to confide – a worry shared is a worry more than halved and if your partner can step up with practical solutions, it once again brings you closer.

After that, sex is the ultimate way to calm you down. It shows you're there for each other and offers a promise that you'll stay. The effect's not just emotional: sex triggers the hormone oxytocin, whose message to brains and bodies is: "Don't worry… you're safe".

Using sex to create security is both instinctive and effective. Consider, then, the possibility of stretching out and allowing yourself to be pleasured into a more relaxed and confident mood.

Irritation: a natural response when life isn't delivering what we want. The problem is, society prefers a happy face and so we push our frustrations down and try not to show any impatience we may be feeling.

But not expressing discontent is one of nature's most effective anaphrodisiacs. Deny anger and it turns sullen and resentful; continue to deny it and over time you kill desire.

There is another way. If it is handled safely, fury can rouse. This doesn't mean violence or even hurtful comments. It does mean that angry energy let loose to an unthreatened lover frees up passion; and that sexual energy expressed with love dissipates ill-temper.

So, next time irritation flares within either of you, tussle on the sofa. Wrestle each other to the bedroom (*see* page 50). Then yell your fury during climax and collapse – anger drained – into your lover's arms.

The all-body hug

Sexologist David Schnarch says that the best way for partners to connect emotionally is to hug. He means more than the glaringly obvious. The Schnarch embrace is a carefully formulated physical connection that, if regularly performed, creates a passionate bond.

Each of you stands comfortably, just a little way apart. You put your arms around each other so your whole bodies touch. You each focus on yourself and how you're feeling. And then you keep hugging until you're both relaxed.

This isn't as simple as it sounds. You'll often be tempted to lean in and put all your weight on your beloved. You'll often be tempted to move away and disengage. And while you're busy wrestling with temptation, your partner will be doing the same.

You will each have to cope not only with what you are feeling, but what you are sensing your partner is feeling. You'll have to accommodate their pulling, their pushing, their withdrawing, or their clinging on. And that in itself will affect you — making you perhaps feel abandoned or pressured. Do you then stand firm and stable, or do you wobble? The hug becomes a microcosm of your relationship.

The ultimate aim is to stand on your own two feet but stay connected with each other, neither to lean nor pull away. Do this and you'll get a sense of what real love is about — being in a relationship with your partner, but at the same time being very much your own person.

You won't, says Schnarch, get this right the first time, or indeed the next several times. But keep going. Regularly, spend a few minutes hugging until you feel secure both in yourself and with your partner. It will, no question, reinforce your love. Over time it will also deepen your desire.

SENSITIVE HANDS

You explore each other's bodies
fully. The joy is not just in being
touched, not only in the
touching, but also in sensing
the other's pleasure.

Romantic touch

No one size fits all. So personalising how you touch in bed means you're not only a skilled lover but also one who's in love enough to learn.

He in particular may need to learn tenderness. Pumping thrusts rarely work for her until right at the end – and often not even then. Instead brush, stroke, caress, tease. Work from extremities to centre. Touch and then withdraw. Open her out, then make her wait and yearn to be opened more. For her, there's rarely any such thing as too much foreplay.

She, meanwhile, may need to learn the joy of direct contact. For him, light touch can be distracting. Instead, keep things brisk and faster than you may think – even if counterpointed by stimulation on mouth, testicles, and nipples. Pausing occasionally gives a unique set of sensations, but inspired handwork is often relentless.

The short cut to mastery is simple: show and tell, look and learn. Romance doesn't mean that you know everything about each other from day one; romance means being willing to observe your lover at the most intimate of moments. Real romance, of course, is being vulnerable enough to let your lover observe you.

Reading the signs

We all signal pleasure. We do it consciously when we urge each other on, hold each other closer, put more energy into our lovemaking. These are clear signals; no debate, no ignoring them.

Where it gets interesting is when our unconscious communicates, when as loving partners we slowly learn to read our beloved's unconscious signals.

"Read" is perhaps the wrong word. We sometimes do all this visually; more often we listen and sense.

Listening, we register shifts in breath speed and depth; a drop in voice tone, a speed-up — if we are close enough to notice — in heart rate.

Sensing, we'll notice a change in body heat and skin texture — muscle tone shifts as we get more aroused. Plus, moisture: obvious as lubrication in all our sensitive parts, but arousal boosts all body fluids.

Those are the universal signals; then there are the customized codes. Every couple has their own; every individual develops new ones when they join a new couple. The particular voice tone meaning "do it more"; the particular flinch when something's not working; the particular shift of weight that proposes a move to your favourite position.

All interesting. More than that, all useful. Don't just note; interpret. Learn what each signal means. What tells you she needs deeper kisses? Which move says he wants a helping hand with his erection? Which signs mean "yes, now" and which mean "not yet"?

There are no rules here, no dictionary of meanings. You need to do the homework, motivated by desire, to turn your lovemaking into a wordlessly choreographed dance.

Breasts

Like buttocks, these, at least in her, are designed to fill the "full of the hand". This could, of course, be her hand as well as his – "offering" her breasts to him is a beautifully romantic gesture and if she follows up by finger-stimulating her nipples, he can be brought to the brink just by the sight alone.

(Fascinatingly, the pleasure isn't only short-term; a German study suggests that gazing at a woman's breasts for ten minutes a day can add five years to a man's life. A good excuse if ever there was one.)

Touching her breasts will, of course, further bring him on. Best is anything that lets him mould; he needs to have them give under his hands. What she needs here is likely to be softer than what he prefers; if there's a big mismatch, get her to lead the way, with his hand over hers to learn directly what plays.

As a variation, she can use them to massage his genitals. Or get him kneeling, her sitting, and one or the other holding her breasts together around his penis. If he climaxes like this, he gives her what is delightfully known as a "pearl necklace".

For her, breast pleasure may be ambiguous; sensation varies with her mood and the time of the month. Some women have an absolute hotline from breast to clitoris; others need encouragement. It may help if the skin is taut, so she could try holding her arms above her head. Try creating a sensual "bridge" by working on her clitoris and nipples simultaneously; over time, the associations will build.

For her pleasure, he can swirl fingers over her breast, use one finger around and around, or give a flat-

palm massage, which Tantric practitioners say
energizes her hormones. Try a slight pinch on the
nipple, swift for one sensation, or held firm then
let go slowly for a different, deeper rush.

He'll instinctively want to move to mouthwork
and that will suit her, too. Tongue around and
around the breast; a lick across each nipple; sucking
movements; a gentle bite.

Don't forget he has breasts as well, though they're
probably less sensitive. She can try with the flat of
her hand, little finger circles around his nipples, or
sucking and licking – though he may not get the
same direct genital link from these manoeuvres
that she does. She could, however, create a bridge for
him by fondling his nipples with one hand or using
her tongue, while working his penis or testicles at
the same time. This may not play but, if it does, the
link thus established could develop a rather nice
long-term response.

Handwork for her

Back in the Middle Ages, Geoffrey Chaucer
(of *Canterbury Tales* fame) believed that the "C word"
that we now shrink from using originally meant
"skilfully designed". That would describe it nicely, a
smorgasbord of different structures — labia, vagina,
clitoris — that give a whole range of possibilities.

He should start by pressing down on her mound of
Venus; around and around with the flat of the palm,
or lightly tugging her pubic hair. Pull back on her
mound then, or use one hand to hold her labia apart
while two fingers of the other hand — or, of course,
a softly applied vibrator — work their way around.

The clitoris needs most attention. Lubricating is key —
it doesn't do it naturally — but it only takes a moment
to dip down to the vagina for some natural moisture.

After that, it's worth remembering that although
the Japanese word for male masturbation means a

hundred rubs, the equivalent word for female means a thousand. There are no short cuts here.

Down the clitoral shaft; just as with the penis, he should take care until it hardens and expands. Nor should he pull back the hood yet – finger work is usually too strong for the exposed glans – best wait and use the tongue.

Perhaps now a detour to the U-spot, newly located by expert scientists; expert lovers, of course, have long known that this tiny area just below the clitoris is a treasure. He can use two fingers, a well-applied knuckle or – best of all – the tip of the soft or erect penis. Combine with breast or ear licking for an orgasm that is subtly sweeter than the usual.

On to her vagina. Let's be clear about this: it can be an irrelevance. Many women won't climax from vaginal stimulation alone, so finger penetration needs to be an accompaniment to clitoral work, not a replacement for it.

That said, as an accompaniment, it can be delicious. He can slide one or two fingers in and then up toward her belly to find her G-spot, then massage it. Sliding farther in again, he will find her A-spot and then her cervix. He should move slowly as he builds her pleasure.

Handwork for him

She should follow her instincts. Human hands will naturally curl around the shaft of a penis and, once there, naturally slide up and down. (However long-term you are as partners, this is always a wonderful way to start.)

From there it's a simple step for her to add a slight twist on the up or down stroke, or to use one hand gently and then the other sharply, or to open out the fists to flat palms and roll the penis between them. Think Demi Moore at her potter's wheel in *Ghost*.

When her attention turns to his glans, she can continue to play. Her whole palm, lubricated, slides curving over the top. Her finger and thumb easing up his foreskin — if it is present — then holding it as tight as purse-strings while she works.

Her hand can grip just below the groove to hold the skin back. The tip of one finger can massage his frenulum, that "little bridge" of skin between glans and shaft; it responds better to stretching rather than friction, so she should move methodically and carefully.

For added sensation, she can divert to his testicles — but carefully, for obvious reasons. She can cup them, hold them lightly, tap them, slide a fingertip along the scored centre line, or grip the whole sac with one hand and pull down. That final manoeuvre, by the way, will more or less double the sensation of whatever she's doing with her other hand.

ORAL
PLEASURE

The touch of lips on skin —
kissing, licking, tasting, and
being tasted. Pure pleasure, pure
sensation, pure intimacy.

Five mouth moves

The lips and tongue are among the most sensitive parts of the body. Which rather explains why oral love is not only a pleasure to receive but also to give. It's also an act of pure intimacy, tasting our lover and letting them taste us is one of the most personal things one can do. Here's a brief tour of the oral possibilities.

1. **Blowing:** stimulates the skin and alters temperature, thus handily firing two sets of nerves at once. Wet the skin with your tongue, sprinkled water, or an erotic spray for extra effect; if you want more steam than you can produce, use a hairdryer. This is particularly effective on the ears and hairline; avoid the vagina, blowing in there can kill.

   Note, though, that for some men blowing is distracting, so it can be usefully used on the penis to slow things down.

2. **Biting:** gently done, raises your endorphin levels,
   though equally is a turn-off if done too hard. He's
   likely to be more into this than she is, but she should
   still cover teeth with lips when nibbling "down there"
   to avoid making him nervous.

   (On the other hand, Dr Charley Ferrer, in her lovely
   book *The Latina Kama Sutra*, suggests that if you bite a
   man's organ just hard enough to make him cringe
   he'll never be unfaithful to you; an interesting
   approach.) What's called a love "bite" is actually
   a suck; *see* next paragraph.

3. **Sucking:** conventionally a move used on him by her,
   but equally wonderful if he sucks her clitoris, though
   he needs to go lighter than she can. Don't ignore other
   protrusions, tongues, nipples, toes. Also the way
   to mark a lover, *à la cannibale*; check first that it's
   acceptable, then suck hard rather than biting. If
   it comes up too bruised, rub firmly, then apply ice
   and cover with a green tinted concealer.

4. **Licking:** tongue work has the advantage over handwork of arriving already lubricated, so you can use it on even the most sensitive of organs. Try long, flat movements or lap regularly with the tip of the tongue; short strokes like the flickering of a flame work well for both him and her. An easily aroused partner with strong memories of your delivering loving oral sex can be driven crazy in public if you trigger those memories by licking your lips while staring at them.

5. **Probing:** do it soft-tongued on genitals; use sharp-tongued on concave venues such as the navel and ear. She may climax from ear probing alone, particularly if it is interspersed with the irregular breath produced by whispering. That said, some women hate it; the same goes for a tongue in the vagina, so check.

    She may use her own probing tongue to call his speed during intercourse. Pace is all here: faster, slower, rhythmic, or arrhythmic can turn a "take it or leave it" move into an orgasm-creator.

Mouthwork for her

The ultimate gift, allowing her to lie back and be worshipped. Wu Hu, Chinese empress of the Tang dynasty, insisted that visiting dignitaries paid homage to her this way; a modern lover could do worse than honour his lady similarly.

If he's taking charge, he should get her sitting while he lies between her thighs, or raise her legs over his shoulders – if done on the edge of the bed, with her hanging over, the rush of blood to her head can produce interesting sensations.

If it's she who wants to control, then she can go on top, kneeling over his face; if you are on the bed or floor, position the whole thing near a wall, so she can lean forward and take the weight on her hands.

He can give licks on her labia, then tiny circles around her U-spot. As for the clitoris, the tongue is the perfect instrument here: warm, delicate, and

above all wet; try working around clockwise
and registering where there's most reaction.

Then he can ease back her clitoral hood and work
carefully to bring her glans erect. Sideways flicks
will usually play here, with an irregular rather than
a steady beat.

Her taste

A word to him directly about her taste. Despite
the wonderful self-descriptions in the theatrical
Vagina Monologues ("Cinnamon and cloves… deep
deep forest… the South Pacific… a brand new
morning… the ocean… God"), sadly, some
women get anxious about the whole thing.

If you love her flavour, love her enough to tell
her so. Even better, touch her, then lick your
own fingers appreciatively so she knows you
mean what you're saying.

Mouthwork for him

For him, a gift, too – of pure pleasure but also acceptance. When she takes him in her mouth, he feels the centre of the world; every man should experience that occasionally.

If she's happy to kneel before him, fine. If it makes her feel unequal, she can seat herself on the bed-edge and have him stand in front, or sit him back against bed pillows while she lies between his legs. Legend has it that concubines used to approach the Sultan for just this purpose by wriggling from the foot of the bed under the bedclothes.

Once there, what to do? The slang term is inaccurate – blowing is a very small part of it, though if she does, across the glans will work best; she should lick first for maximum effect of cool breath on wet skin. Or use long licks on the shaft, then hold firm, with the foreskin pulled gently back as she kisses with closed mouth, then opens and takes him in.

For expert work it's best to keep the tongue constantly in motion — flat, tensed, rolled, around and around, or flicking across the tiny string-like frenulum at his tip. Any of these combined with an occasional strong suck will push most men over the edge.

She can also kiss his testicles, take them into her mouth, suck, lick, and probe (carefully) with a stiff tongue.

If she's willing to accommodate him deeply, use a position in which he's facing her feet; that way his penis follows the natural curve of her throat and everything follows nicely.

His taste

A word to her directly about swallowing. You don't have to. It's a wonderful, loving gesture and, if you do, he'll appreciate your intention. But if you really hate the idea, there are other options.

So instead, as he starts to tip over — his penis swells, his testicles pull up, you can feel fluid oozing from his glans — then quickly shift position so that you are obliging with your hand, but he is climaxing away from your mouth. Across your breasts is a thoughtful and easy to arrange gesture, or simply over your hands while you move to kiss him elsewhere.

If you want to follow through, but just don't like the sensation, then one way to make it easier is to take him in deeply then swallow all in one go so it doesn't hit your tongue. If you're not keen on deep, then pop your tongue over his penis so he climaxes under it and avoids the taste buds.

If it's his taste that's the problem, it's loving rather than critical to let him know. If the issue is hygiene, then institute a ritual of bathing together first. If neither that nor a medical checkup helps, it could be his diet — suggest he eats more fruit. Pineapple, apparently, makes all the difference.

Tongue bath

A wonderful one-way attention to mark a special occasion with an offering of warm, wet pleasure. The receiver lies comfortably, first face down, then on their back; the giver covers with tongue strokes every square inch of skin — hence the nickname "a trip around the world".

Light and quick, long and slow, pausing at each erogenous zone. Lips and nipples, obviously; less obviously, the ears, eyelids, toes. This one won't play if you make it rough — it needs to be the ultimate in gentle attention. If the giver's mouth gets dry, they can keep a glass of water nearby or lightly bite their tongue to get saliva flowing.

The traditional end stage is to return to your partner's mouth, then work your way down their centre line — detouring only at the nipples — to reach your final destination with extended tongue work.

Your signature move

Developing a variation that's not just memorably arousing, but also something your lover has only ever had from you. By definition, you need to create this recipe for yourself. The ingredients you use, however, are definable.

You could use a regular move but on an unexpected body part — sucking on fingers or toes, or licking under arms. Or choose a regular target for oral sex, but use a different move from normal: he could write his name on her breasts with his tongue, she could probe rhythmically around his glans, with an extra flourish when she reaches the frenulum.

You could use a different or varying rhythm: slow, slow, quick, quick slow across glans or clitoris. Or combine favoured moves in a different way: he could lick her while slowly rubbing the sole of her foot, she could lick him while imprinting nail marks on his buttocks.

You could use added extras. Ice chips under the tongue; brandy held in the mouth; toothpaste on the lips — though only a little (too much stings). And that's not even going the route of dedicated lubricants by the shelf full in sex stores and on websites, to soothe, warm, or tingle.

If you need motivation here, consider the memorable tale of the woman who first produced her signature move on her honeymoon, when she pleasured her new husband for an hour non-stop, finishing up with a spectacular combination of lips, tongue, and breasts. Apparently he fell in love with her all over AGAIN — and he was besotted to begin with.

In short, the art is first to find a manoeuvre that's achingly memorable but is also new to your partner, then to reserve it, your mutual secret.

It's a moving gift to make sure that you never do this particular move with anyone else ever again.

UNION

As your limbs entwine,
desire takes over. As your
bodies thrust, passion builds.
There has never been a
better time than this.

Romantic penetration

That unique moment. She trusts herself enough to open. He trusts enough to be enveloped; penis and vagina seem then to belong to both.

You both need to be ready. She needs to be fully aroused — clitoris and labia will signal as they swell, while the vagina's opening is usually shown by her lubrication. Check with a finger, though it's always worthwhile adding more.

It may help at the start for her to penetrate herself with one or more fingers, circling slightly to stretch all the muscles.

If it's him who's not quite prepared, a little mouthwork usually does the trick. But he doesn't need to be as readily erect as one may think — going in soft often gets the desired result simply because being inside is so much more arousing for him than being outside.

Whichever way penetration happens, it's courteous to let her guide his entry, hands on buttocks. If she's wary – perhaps for a first time together – let her go on top and lower herself down to her own schedule.

But him thrusting in urgently can be just as delicious, though with a rather different tone. Best done by long-term couples and when she's very aroused – again, extra lubrication may be needed.

Re-entry, of course, will be a different matter entirely; moving from one position to another will typically make it more welcome each time for her, particularly if you use positions for which her legs are wide and her vagina stretched. (If the issue is that she is overstretched, try legs together.)

The most important things here, though, aren't the postures, the movements, or the timing. The most important thing is the feeling of being together, absolutely as one.

Safety and protection

Not the most romantic of topics, but surely a sign of love. If you really care, you won't want to be giving your partner, or yourself, an infection or an unexpected baby. So, even if she's on the pill, unless both of you have been tested, you'll use a condom.

If you do use a condom, a nice gesture is for her to place it on with her mouth.

1. Remove any lipstick or gloss, otherwise the oil will break down the latex.

2. Lube lips with clear, water-based lubricant and add more in the nipple end of the condom.

3. Hold the nipple between thumb and forefinger, edges flipped out, and then circle with lips.

4. Hold the penis shaft in one hand and kiss the glans.

5. Wrap lips over teeth then push condom firmly but gently down to fit.

The matrimonial

Him-on-top, the position so classic – and so classically romantic – that Tuscan lovers used to call it the "angelic position". Face-to-face, so endlessly good for touching, talking, kissing.

Good, too, for orgasms, particularly with her legs curved around his waist and pulling him in close. It's perfect for post-coital cuddling, too; with him still inside, each can hold the other close and easily fall asleep entwined.

Also, it's highly adaptable. Alter how deep he goes by shifting the height of her legs from flat to over his shoulders – the higher the legs, the deeper the penetration. Alter her tightness by shifting how close together her legs are – try crossing her ankles for maximum effect. Alter connection by shifting his angle over her: fully forward, his pubic bone will give her stronger sensations, while leaning away his arched back will do the same for him.

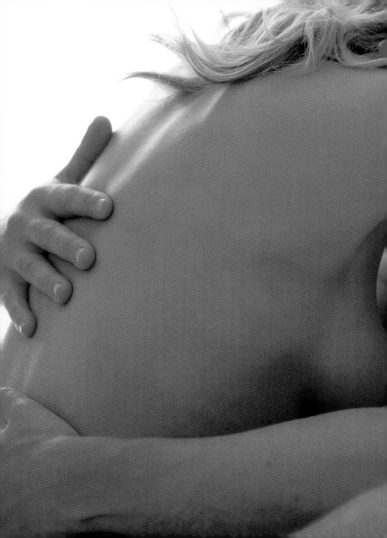

Also good is the fact that the matrimonial works
in almost any location that provides a firm surface —
so use your imagination and never limit yourselves
to the bed.

That said, even the bed offers variations. She can go
legs over the edge with him standing in front, or
both can lie across with her head dropping down.
Add a few pillows or he can raise her buttocks with
his hands — tiring for her, but adds a whole new level
of sensation for both of you.

The only time matrimonial doesn't play well for her
is if she feels over-controlled and somehow "pinned
down"; not the most loving of experiences. He can
help by taking more weight on his arms and letting
her control the moves.

The only time matrimonial doesn't play well
for him is if it triggers too early a climax. Shallow
versions will offset the problem or he can use
other positions first and turn her to finish.

Upper hands

Her equivalent of matrimonial; she gets to take charge and (often) orgasm speedily.

Can be best for him because he can relax and not over-exert, which will slow him down — and he can enjoy her display. Can be best for her if she doesn't mind being the one on display. (Given the current near-universal anxiety about body image, a loving partner at this point reassures her that she looks very beautiful and turns him on very much.)

Once he's fully stiffened — by her hands and mouth if necessary — she can lower herself on to him as slowly as pleases her and then take any position, facing in any direction.

The basic movement is up and down, but she can also go side-to-side, back and forth, circling with her hips — and she can lean down toward him or away from him to the point where she is lying fully back.

She can also adjust depth. With her knees up, she can take only the tip of his penis and combine that with a tiny movement to stimulate just the first inch of her vagina and his glans alone. With her knees down each side of his chest and her thighs spread, she can take him in as deep as she (and he) likes.

Each variation feels different; if willing to orchestrate, she can create quite a symphony. Plus, her own symphony's enhanced because she or he can easily touch almost any part of her: he can even reach her buttocks if she leans well enough forward or turns around.

The only problem is that this isn't the most stable of positions; she needs to keep firmly fixed. Columbian tribes used to avoid it for this very reason because in their world if a woman lost connection during intercourse, the world would tumble into the cosmic waters and be lost for ever. A nice implication.

Side-by-side

This is just as intimate as matrimonial and with even more body contact — yet is much more relaxing, particularly if he's tired. Tantric masters recommended it as a cool-down after more energetic sex.

Side-by-side and face-to-face gives the ultimate in shallow penetration if you want to make it last. Plus, it means her vagina curls tightly around the penis, so it's also the ultimate for keeping him erect — try it particularly if he's already taken a few orgasms and needs help to manage one more.

In this situation, try it even if you aren't optimistic — she wraps her leg around his waist to guide the process and keep him in place. Then let her internal grip and some gentle mutual movements resolve the issue one way or another.

Side-by-side with him behind — the "spoons" position — has even more possibilities. Either he or she can touch breasts or clitoris; make this even easier by his rolling slightly onto his back, taking her with him.

To add yet more sensation she can lean forward and him away to form a wide V; his penis then comes in at just the right angle for good G-spot stimulation.

Remember the clitoris

Let's not, in this rush for penetration, sideline that small but very powerful structure which, on average, has something like 6000 nerve endings — over twice as many as his relevant organ.

Because the clitoris is her relevant organ. Whereas his intercourse pleasure hinges on the connection between penis and vagina, the reverse isn't necessarily true. Scientists now know that it's the clitoris, not the vagina, that is her penis equivalent; it's that which is going to need most attention.

This can demand flexibility when it comes to intercourse; the penetration that works for him may not do much for her. But there are ways.

First option: he can use hand or mouth to nudge her to the edge and only then penetrate; some easily stimulatable women can then survive the shift to intercourse and continue on up the arousal curve.

Second option: you can choose penetration positions that get the clitoris involved. See what works for your particular configuration; some positions, for some women, do it either directly or by stretching her labia or hitting her G-spot. Experiment; the CAT position (*see* page 172) looks especially promising.

The third — and by no means least-romantic — option: add in extra stimulation during intercourse. He or she reaches down with hand, fingertip, or wand vibrator; the crucial positions here are her-on-top or from behind, leaving clear space for easy access. All the above, though, will work only when everyone's relaxed and she in particular is confident.

A final note. Never think her odd if she doesn't come through penetration alone; if she can't, she's absolutely normal. Bottom line: if she can bring herself to climax solo, then as a couple your task is to acknowledge that there are ways and then recreate those ways as a duet.

The pompoir

Not so much a position as a skill she can use to keep him hard – known in the *Kama Sutra* as the "Mare's Trick". Her vaginal muscles don't just grip his penis but actively massage, caress, and even ripple around it.

He gets excellent enjoyment and she gets more lubrication, a stronger orgasm, and good control –

if she's really skilful she can draw him in and up
to the precise point inside where she wants him.

All this doesn't come without some work. She'll
need to practise what are currently known as Kegel
exercises, squeezing the muscles that come into
play when she passes water. Try 40 repetitions a
day to start with – doable during the day at her desk
or while commuting; better, of course, practised
during the night around the real thing.

Slow passion

The ultimate in romantic sex – long and leisurely,
with extended pauses to gaze into each other's eyes.

Best for all this are positions of shallow penetration
that hold him back. So lie on your sides facing each
other, or try matrimonial but with her legs close
together. Bring her along with a hand to her clitoris –
or break off so that he can lick her, then insert again.

When you're both on the edge, he keeps the whole thing balanced with circular grinding or alternating short, sharp strokes with long, slow ones. If she can handle pauses without losing momentum, he can also stop for a few heartbeats until she gets desperate for more and arches in to bring him on again.

Quick lust

Sex taken on the run when there's very little time to spare — sheer speed gives excitement that can make it just as romantic as the slow version. Traditionally done outdoors when the mood strikes, but often nicer at home, while getting dressed for work or before friends arrive for supper.

The short time schedule — according to one American study, a quickie averages seven minutes — demands specific technique. He goes deep, fast, and forceful, using an upright matrimonial position for preference and — if she can bear it — leaving out the lubrication in the interests of friction.

He can get a fair orgasm; she may have to wait. To make equal shares more likely, she could help herself out by hand — ideally keeping time with his thrusts.

Relaxed love

Not simply an unstressed session, but one in which you take your orgasms with absolutely no effort at all; gives a melting rather than exploding climax.

The theory here is that the whole sound and fury of intercourse can sometimes be just too much — bodies go into overdrive and lovers lose that crucial connection. Taking the effort out of it all aims to allow you to feel the sensations more deeply, to be aware of yourselves and each other rather than of the relentless drive toward orgasm.

The practice, as opposed to the theory, is that you both need to arouse yourselves in any appropriate way but preferably with long foreplay and a gentle approach. Take a position you're both comfortable with, one where you can stay still for long periods — side-by-side would play well.

Then, as you approach the edge, stop all movement. Don't try to do anything or, indeed, not do anything. Relax and let your bodies take over.

You may find yourselves moving instinctively, or not moving at all; either will do if it focusses you not on performance but on what you're feeling here and now.

This is not easy to master because the temptation is to continue regardless. It'll help to practise first; let one of you offer hand and mouthwork to the other, who then learns how to let go and not try.

It's worth the effort in the end, however; it feels indescribably loving. Expect tearfulness.

On the threshold

However you play intercourse — fast, slow, relaxed, urgent — there comes a point just before climax when everything focusses.

The plateau phase, the point at which the balance of pleasure and romance is greatest. You're as aroused as you can be without orgasm, yet still aware of your partner. The feeling of connection is very deep.

How to build on this? Don't try to prolong the moment — it will happen at its own speed. But do learn to recognize it when it happens and, when it does happen, turn to your partner and simply cling on. (While your partner, who has learned over time to recognize the signs of your approaching orgasm, simply clings on to you, too.)

Knowing that in just a few seconds you are going to orgasm, knowing that your beloved knows it, knowing that they are holding you as you tip over… Once experienced, that moment is never forgotten.

COMING

In the moment of orgasm,
you cling together. It's in this
instant that love is made.

Romantic climax

The Japanese word for orgasm means "to go somewhere else". That sounds about right to me. Not just because of the pleasure, but also the sense that you're so at one as a couple that you've left your own bodies and become part of each other's. (The French expression *la petite mort* or "little death" is more dramatic, but the sense is the same.)

Physically, this idea of unity is absolutely correct. Her orgasm and his are precisely similar (but she, happily, can have more spasms). In a test, men and women wrote descriptions of their peaks — experts had no idea which climax belonged to which gender. You may be different people, but you are loving partners having the same experience.

There is a way to increase that sense of oneness — a way that only 10 per cent of people regularly follow but maybe more should try. It's simply this:

to climax with your eyes open. You look at your partner, your partner looks at you. (It's David Schnarch again who recommends this, calling it not "eye contact", but "I contact".)

It sounds scary — we're not used to being so vulnerable. We tend to think we look ugly at orgasm and we may need to be reminded that uncontrolled passion is even more beautiful than self-controlled elegance. Plus, we're not used to having to concentrate on someone else; we need to let direct gaze bring us closer, not put us off our game.

Climaxing open-eyed isn't learnable by force of will. But practice will help: each time you make love, keep your eyes open for longer and longer.

Once you have mastered it, seeing a partner's passion will arouse rather than distract you. In time, the idea of a partner seeing your passion will mean feeling accepted rather than nervous.

Orgasm for him

A secret very few men will admit, and so very few women know, is this: making it good for him can sometimes be a case of releasing him from having to make it good for her.

Yes, of course most of the time he'll want to pay her attention; that's what love is. Which is exactly why, just occasionally, the most romantic gift a woman can give her partner is what one might call a "duty-free" orgasm.

If he's taking the lead, she can tell him at the start that this one's all for him, that he can do it at exactly the speed, rhythm, and pressure he wants. Her job thereafter is to match him, go with him, support him in taking exactly the positions he wants, precisely reflect his moves with hers.

If it's she who's doing the work, she can take total responsibility so he doesn't have to. Kissing his lips,

sucking his nipples, then working with hand and mouth on his penis, testicles, and perineum. To keep his absolute full attention, she should keep shifting the rhythm. Then, she should ride him – he, lying back with no other task than to focus utterly on his own pure pleasure.

Her final gift would be to notice the window of opportunity when he passes the point of no return (it lasts five seconds, so don't blink). In that moment, she should take all responsibility and focus everything on him, simply letting him enjoy his orgasm for himself alone.

Orgasm for her

A secret that has just recently come to light, and so few women and even fewer men know it, is this: making it good for her is largely a matter of helping her feel secure.

Neuroscientist Gert Holstege's recent research suggests that only when women are emotionally relaxed enough to switch off the fear centres of their brains can they climax. Which is why, almost always, the most romantic gift a man can give his partner is to help her feel safe.

This isn't solely a matter of heaping on pure physical sensation – unlike his, her brain doesn't turn off anxiety as it turns on arousal. The reassurances romance offer may be optional for him; for her they are almost always essential. She needs foreplay that's emotional as well as physical – words, gestures, cuddles, affection.

Follow up with lots of gentle touching; bringing her skin alive with head-to-foot caresses, alternating between clitoris and vagina to trigger two sets of sensations that will short circuit any temptation to tense up. Loving words from him will help her relax and, crucially, make her feel beautiful and desired.

Unless she's nervous about her own performance, it may also help to let her take charge. She could lead her first orgasm herself with his attention, follow up with an intercourse climax with her on top, take her final peak with him licking and her directing – "stop... start... now".

The positive postscript is this: the more orgasms she has with a lover, the more she's likely to have. The security that comes with knowing she can climax creates a virtuous spiral that makes it a thousand times more likely that she'll climax again.

Come again

Given that she probably can and he isn't guaranteed to be able to, it's loving to schedule things to take care of you both.

So if she likes penetration and he knows that once is – for him – enough, he may offer to delay his orgasm until the very end. En route to that end, he can give her one or two more orgasms using his hands and mouth, or her sex toy of choice.

Alternatively, she may offer to put in all the energy to begin with, then take her orgasms any which way once he's satisfied.

Don't assume, however, that once he's done, he's done; it's amazing what dedicated affection and a lack of pressure can achieve. Sometimes all he needs to hear is, "Don't worry… it's fine" for the dead to come back to life again.

Don't assume, either, that just because she can physiologically break records, she wants to. She may want to hold back and back for one huge finale much like his.

As always – it doesn't need saying, really – treat every occasion as a new event and discuss together what feels right for this time.

COMING
TOGETHER

You balance each other's
pleasure, arousal moving
from one to the other
then back again. Suddenly,
you're both on fire.

Simultaneous climax

Of course, this is the ideal. Truly passionate, truly romantic — of course every truly loving couple reaches the peak at the same time, every single time.

Except, actually, they don't.

So many of us aim for it — but the hard truth is that simultaneous orgasms are a rare and exotic creature. If you've never had one you're absolutely typical; if you have them regularly you are special indeed.

If you've tried to have one, but failed, it probably means that you were uncomfortably divided between getting pleasure for yourself in pursuit of your own climax and giving pleasure to your partner in pursuit of theirs. The result is a double-bind and the main reason why simultaneous orgasm is so tricky to achieve.

So, however romantic it seems to come together, if you haven't and you can't, don't fret.

Instead, maximize what you have. Take turns and make one session for him, the next for her. Take sequential orgasms, by hand, mouth, penetration, and then around the circle again. Take your own peaks, but together.

Bottom line: so long as there are roughly equal shares between you, what matters isn't whether you're simultaneous. What matters is that you're making love.

Speeding

All that said, if you do want to achieve simultaneous orgasms, then there are ways. No promises for every time or even regularly — but the secret is twofold. First, you need to speed up the slower partner (usually her). Second, you need to slow down the faster partner (often him). Balance these and you multiply your chances of success.

Accelerate her by starting way in advance of the act:
fantasies a few days beforehand… foreplay that
morning without a climax allowed… sensuous
phone calls in the lunch hour… romantic texts
on her way home.

Once she gets home, she needs sensitive work on
her favourite erogenous zones by hand, mouth, or
vibrator, while she deepens her breathing, tilts her
pelvis, exaggerates her noise – the proven ways
of signalling to her body to prepare for climax.

Aim, in everything, for maximum lubrication –
which handily brings her nearer to the edge but
keeps him back by reducing friction.

Get her utterly on the edge but not climaxing – or,
if this makes orgasm more certain, get her taking
a couple of preparatory ones to signal to her body
what's in store. She needs to be absolutely ready
before you carry on.

Slowing

Meanwhile, hold him back. How? Don't even think about the advertised "desensitizing" creams; they dull his sensations and, by association, dull hers. Equally, ignore the mental exercises that aim to distract him by making him less aware of his arousal; they also make him less likely to spot when he's going to come and so less able to avoid the whole problem.

More effective is for either her or him gently to press two fingers just below his glans to soften his erection and set him back.

Or he can do the "big squeeze", a lovely Tantric move that delays him but also focusses his attention on pleasure. As soon as he feels even near to crisis point, he pulls up as hard as he can, relaxes, and lengthens his neck, takes a deep breath and holds it. He waits, breathes, and, when he feels his arousal lessening, he starts again.

Mouthwork for two

At this point, with you both desirous, ready, and moving to penetration, you may like to stop and consider an alternative. How about mutual oral sex? No, it's not intercourse but, equally, it's not a fake; it is a delicious way of both speeding her to climax and giving her the chance to keep him waiting until she's ready.

Have him on his back and her on top but reversed. Or her lying with her head over the edge of the bed while he leans over her. Or head to tail on their sides, each other's thighs as cushions – the position the original French term *soixante-neuf* (69) referred to.

Let him work a little harder than she does. Let her be prepared to keep him waiting sometimes. Let both stop, start, and play catch-up. Given that, your chances of crossing the finishing line together will be deliciously high.

Helpful positions

If you're wanting simultaneous via intercourse, there's actually a lot you can do with positions.

Side-by-side means shallow thrusting so he slows down. Her-on-top means less body tension for him, which also means he slows down.

For her, the control of being above will bring her along – she can get the deepest penetration by reversing, so that she is facing his feet – and she can double the potential with a helpful hand or vibrator.

But the queen of positions for her speedy orgasm is a new arrival on the block – CAT, the acronym for "coital alignment technique". He goes on top as in the classic matrimonial, but then slides down so his public bone nudges her clitoris.

She then tilts her pelvis with every thrust so that, as he penetrates fully, her clitoris is tugged. This may take some experimentation; try it with her on top first and then, once you've both got the hang of it, you can roll over. The success rate, apparently, is an impressive 77 per cent.

Final suggestions

Two further ideas for if none of the above works.

First, try alternating. She does absolutely what best pleases her until she is near the edge, then hands over the choreography to him. He majors on his preferred moves until he's near to coming, then hands back to her. It takes practice to keep both of you hovering on the brink – but can work well.

Second, if all else fails, just stop trying. For her, in particular, the key to orgasming is usually to relax and let go of any imperatives. So, simply forget about the whole thing. Mysteriously, one day when you are least expecting it and most in tune with each other, it just may happen.

AFTERWARDS

The precious space after orgasm
— a blend of excitement and
exhaustion. Only you know
what you've shared. Only you
know what it means.

A second round

Both now spent, lying in each other's arms.
Do you want to go again?

If so, you may take a while to regroup; he in
particular may want to nap and, if so, his best
option is to sit upright and breathe deeply to
keep his energy high.

She can help by taking over, stiffening him by hand
and mouth or reaching for the vibrator. Then try a
position that allows for soft entry: side-by-side or
with her riding on top while he simply enjoys.

If it's only her who's still eager, he can take his turn
with vibrator work or — if she's getting sore — with
long, slow tongue strokes. If he's too tired to oblige
or she wants quick and reliable, he can hold her
while she does it, timing his love talk to her climax.
(Of course, all that applies in reverse if he's eager
and she's not.)

Or, aim for mutual. The full 69 is probably too demanding for this stage in the proceedings, so lie next to each other or head-to-toe, propped up by cushions, observing while you each bring yourselves along. There's something very beautiful about watching a beloved arouse themselves and feeling your own pleasure build at the same time.

Winding down

Truly finished, either of you — but particularly he — may be exhausted not only by the exercise, but also by the rush of post-coital hormones signalling that you're done.

At which point, nature's suggestion is to sleep. But if you must get up and get going, then either take a colder-than-normal shower after sex, or drink coffee half an hour before it; the caffeine hit should kick in at just the right point to offset the post-coital dip.

That said, some folk have a natural upsurge of energy. In her this may mean wanting to talk, hug, interact — in him it's more likely to mean bouncing out of bed, at which point she can feel stranded. So it's vital to take a little time to cuddle, compliment, connect. It's a good move on both counts — the interaction will reassure her emotionally and the skin-on-skin contact will calm him down.

Best, in all honesty, is to lie touching but not talking. Being physically near, not analysing but simply remembering the powerful experience you've shared will not only bring you emotionally closer but also fix the event in your mind. You are, in the most literal sense, making a memory.

Occasionally there may be tears — usually from her, but from him, too, after a very strong climax or a long period of abstinence. This "post coital tristesse" isn't sadness but a backlash after passion, part release of stress, part come-down from the sexual high.

Let it play out, supported by firm, safe hugs.
The tearful one will come back into balance
sooner than you think.

Sleeping together

It's not just the sex that creates the romance but the
entwining afterward — so even if you're in separate
beds, at least nod off together and leave retreating to
your individual nests until later. These positions will
help keep the connection.

The face-to-face hug: hugely intimate and a favourite
of very new, or recently reunited, couples. You're
absolutely open to each other, near enough to breathe
in each other's odour, kiss, stimulate, penetrate;
because of which it's the position most likely to lead
to a repeat bout.

But that very closeness may mean you can't settle;
in particular, your arms and legs may well end up

uncomfortably fighting for space. Try it until you get sleepy then shift around until you're comfortable.

Spoons: the most common sleeping position for the first three to five years of a relationship. It gives physical intimacy – whoever's behind can reach around and fondle whoever's in front or he can penetrate once more if she's willing to angle forward to help him find his way.

Plus, it offers equality; classically, when one partner turns in sleep, the other follows suit so both "spoon" on the other side. Conversation possibility is low, however, so use this position when you both genuinely want to sleep.

Finally, the royal hug: textbook for long-term couples. He lies on his back, she snuggles into his chest. There's no real genital contact, but it offers mutual attention, eye contact, and the option of talking well into the night; if either does feel like another bout they can reach to touch.

Perfect, too, for if she can't sleep — his heatbeat will soothe her, his scent will make her feel secure. If it's he who can't sleep, they can change position, though he may get a better effect lying across and between her breasts.

A tip relevant to any of the above positions: breathe with each other as you start to doze. It not only relaxes but also reassures you; you'll nod off more quickly and stay asleep more deeply.

Love again

If sleeping together after sex is wonderful, waking to sex is surely twice as lovely.

Particularly good is the unilateral surprise attack — pinning her so she wakes to being licked or stealthily using handwork so he's roused by his developing erection. Not recommended with a new or easily startled lover, but with established partners it's all part of the game — and doubtless the favour will be returned in a day or two. Savour the anticipation!

Good, too, is the session that's planned in advance. Particularly if you know you're time-limited or will be child-interrupted, set the alarm for a clear hour or so before you need to be up and about; add mugs of hot coffee and a trip to the bathroom for breath freshening purposes and then take it slowly. This relaxed lead-in will play particularly well in winter when your biological time clocks may not be set for early-morning romance.

Perhaps best of all is the spontaneous session — at any time of the night, sliding into sex without any input from your conscious minds. (There are three or four windows of erection opportunity during an average sleep period, each lasting about half an hour; plenty of chances there if you want them, though of course lovemaking should be verstatile enough to continue even if he doesn't rise to the occasion.)

Only one question remains: how best to rouse
a sleeping partner?

Unless you know that your beloved adores instant
intercourse, it's wise to begin with gentle foreplay.
Despite his generally more speedy response, this
is as true of him as of her. For either gender, being
woken by sudden penetration can be just too
much too early.

But she can go for direct touch, gentle but insistent;
kissing his eyelids open so that his first sight is her
face, then touching his nipples lightly, before
proceeding downward.

Rather than sight, words are what will most likely
rouse her, so his equivalent is first to whisper in her
ear, then give gentle kisses on neck and mouth.

And then, as you both come awake, the whole
loving game can begin all over again.

Afterword

In the end, it comes down to this. If you love someone, you'll want to make love with them. And if you make love with them, that will build your love.

Of course there'll be times when energy is low and life gets in the way. But with just the smallest slice of motivation, you should be able to move close, reach out, and remember what desire feels like.

When that happens, act on it. Seize the chance and create the opportunity. That is what will keep you close as your relationship deepens. That is what will keep your romance — and your passion — alive and loving in the years ahead.

Acknowledgements

Many thanks to all the wonderful friends and colleagues who have helped make these books happen, particularly to: Nick Comfort, Barbara Levy, Joy Haughton, Laura Bates, Colin Marsh and all the great people at Mitchell Beazley.

Susan Quilliam